I0814191

NORTH AMERICAN FIELD GUIDES

# BATS

Angela Lim

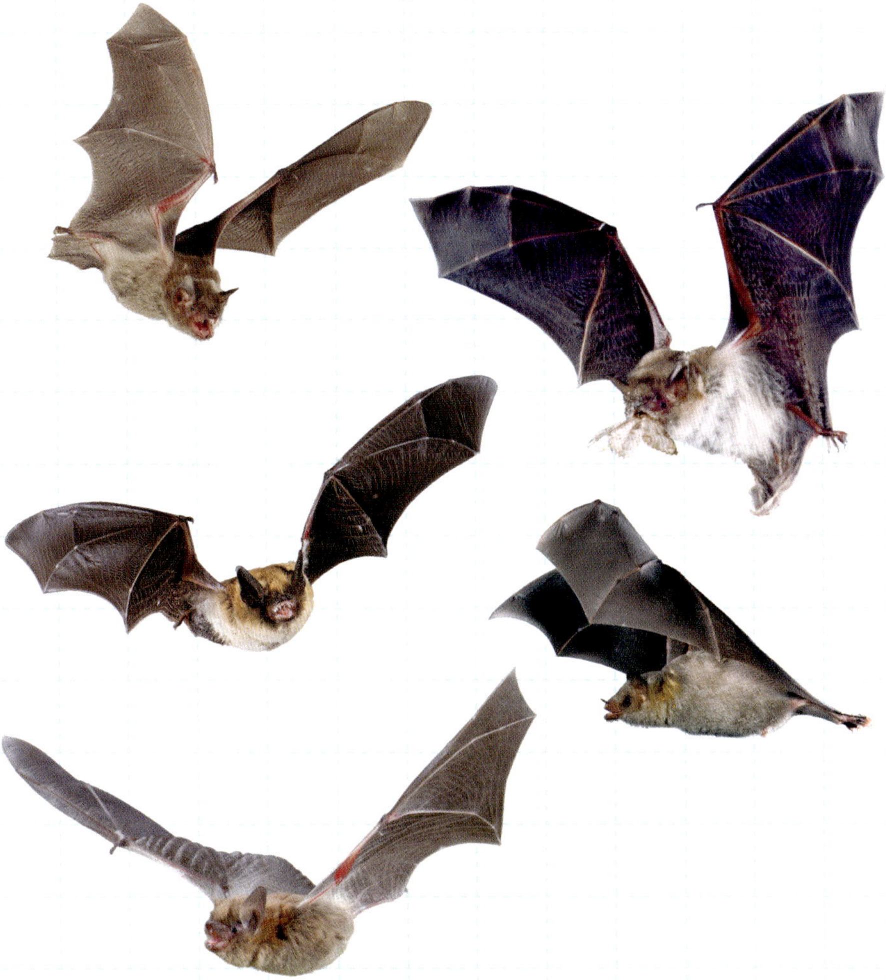

An Imprint of Abdo Reference | abdobooks.com

# CONTENTS

Free-Tailed Bats
Mormoopid Bats
Leaf-Nosed Bats
Vesper Bats

# WHAT ARE BATS?

Bats are a type of mammal. Like other mammals, bats are warm blooded, have fur, and produce milk. Unlike other mammals, bats have wings and can fly. Some mammals can glide, but bats are the only mammals capable of true flight. Most bats drop from their perch to launch into flight. Nearly all bats are nocturnal, meaning they are most active at night.

Bats play important roles in their ecosystems. Some bats are pollinators. Without bats, production of crops such as bananas and avocados would decline. Fruit-eating bats, which can be found in the Pacific Islands, the Caribbean, and Latin America, help spread seeds. Additionally, many bats are insectivores. Some bats eat as many as 600 insects in an hour! Without bats, farms would be overrun with insects. Bat poop, called guano, can be used as fertilizer.

## BAT CATEGORIES

There are 153 bat species native to North America. These bats can be divided into groups called families. Bats in the same family share common features and behaviors. North American bats are grouped into four main families:

- Free-tailed bats belong to the Molossidae family. These bats have bony tails that are not enclosed in membranes.
- Mormoopid bats have stiff hairs on their muzzles that look like mustaches. Bats in the Mormoopidae family have large lips, and the lower lip has several folds. These bats are also known as ghost-faced bats, mustached bats, and naked-backed bats.
- Leaf-nosed bats are named for the spear-like structure that juts upward from the nose. Most species in the Phyllostomidae family have short, wide wings.

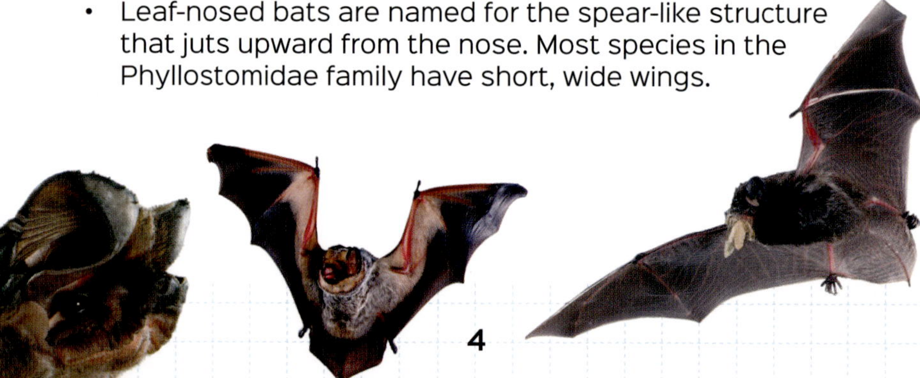

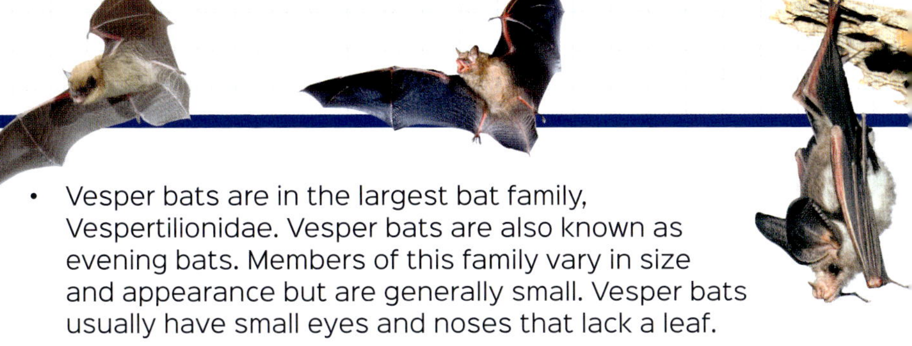

- Vesper bats are in the largest bat family, Vespertilionidae. Vesper bats are also known as evening bats. Members of this family vary in size and appearance but are generally small. Vesper bats usually have small eyes and noses that lack a leaf.

## BAT IDENTIFICATION

Bat species can be identified by specific physical characteristics. Bats have fur that varies in color. A bat's fur may be black, tan, red, gray, or other colors. The shapes of a bat's nose, tail, and ears can help with identification.

Many bats use echolocation while in flight. This means they make high-pitched sounds and listen for how the sound waves bounce off objects such as prey. Each bat species sounds different. A device called a bat detector can be used to analyze the sounds and help identify the species.

In this book, bats are described according to their average adult size and weight. When identifying bats, it is helpful to also note the following characteristics:

- Size: The average wingspan and weight of a bat species.
- Range: The geographic area where a bat species is found.
- Habitat: The type of environment in which a bat species thrives, such as caves, forests, or deserts.
- Diet: The typical food source of a bat species.

Note: When you see bats outside, observe them from a distance, avoid touching them, and be aware of potential risks like rabies.

# HOW TO USE THIS BOOK

Tab shows the bat category.

VESPER BATS

## HOARY BAT *(LASIURUS CINEREUS)*

The hoary bat is a widespread but uncommon bat. The bat has long, soft hair that is dark brown or black at the ... white at the tips, giving the bat ... ce. The hoary bat also has a ... round its face. This coloring makes it ... nging from a tree branch.

The bat's common name appears here.

This paragraph gives information about the bat.

WIND TURBINES

Hoary bats are one of the bat species most heavily affected by wind turbines. These creatures sometimes collide with wind turbines during flight. It is estimated that 76,000 to 152,000 hoary bats are killed due to wind turbine collisions each year. Researchers are looking for ... fety of wind turbines for wildlife. ... ine may make a sound to deter ... e.

66

Sidebars provide additional information about the topic.

The bat's scientific name appears here.

HOW TO SPOT

**Size:** Average wingspan of 17 inches (43.2 cm); 0.7 to 1.2 ounces (19.8 to 34 g)
**North American Range:** Canada through Central America
**Habitat:** Forest edges
**Diet:** Moths and other insects

*How to Spot* boxes give information about the bat's size, range, habitat, and diet.

Images show the bat.

**FUN FACT**
**The hoary bat's long, narrow wings allow it to fly at speeds of up to 13 miles per hour (21 kmh).**

*Fun Facts* give interesting information about bats.

During the winter months, this bat migrates to war habitats. It migrates in groups but roosts alone in old mature trees. These bats change roosts regularly.

Hoary bats mate in the fall just before migrating. However, fertilization is delayed until the following sp Females give birth while hanging upside down in a roosting site. They often have twins.

67

# BIG FREE-TAILED BAT

## *(NYCTINOMOPS MACROTIS)*

The big free-tailed bat has a glossy coat that ranges from dark red to dark brown. The bat has a black face, a thin muzzle, and a wrinkled upper lip. It has forward-facing ears and long, thin wings. Males are slightly larger than females.

The big free-tailed bat is nocturnal. It hunts at night, catching flying and ground-dwelling insects. It usually hunts alone but sometimes hunts in small groups.

Big free-tailed bats are found in temperate and tropical climates in the US Southwest and Mexico. They roost along rocky cliffs and in trees and buildings. These bats migrate, traveling as far north as British Columbia, Canada, in the summer.

Big free-tailed bats mate in the winter. Females give birth to one pup after a gestation period of about two to three months. Young bats are fully grown in four months.

### HOW TO SPOT

**Size:** Wingspan of 16.5 to 17.3 inches (42 to 44 cm); 0.8 to 1.1 ounces (22.7 to 31.2 g)

**North American Range:** Southwestern British Columbia, southwestern United States, Mexico, Cuba, Jamaica, Hispaniola, and Central America

**Habitat:** Rocky, dry landscapes

**Diet:** Large moths, crickets, stink bugs, and flying ants

## WING ANATOMY

A bat's wings extend from its shoulders and ankles out to its fingers. The wings are made of membrane that is tough but flexible. Each wing includes the same arm bones that humans have, such as the humerus, radius, and ulna. Bats have four long fingers and a thumb enclosed in each wing. Most bats have a similar membrane that connects the ankle to the tail. The tails of free-tailed bats extend far beyond this connective membrane.

# MEXICAN FREE-TAILED BAT

## *(TADARIDA BRASILIENSIS)*

Mexican free-tailed bats are medium-sized bats with reddish, dark brown, or gray fur. They have short snouts and wrinkled upper lips. Their forward-pointing ears are black. Mexican free-tailed bats have long, narrow wings. They fly at an average speed of about 60 miles per hour (97 kmh) but can fly as fast as 100 miles per hour (160 kmh).

### HOW TO SPOT

**Size:** Wingspan of 12 to 14 inches (30.5 to 35.6 cm); 0.4 to 0.5 ounces (11.3 to 14.2 g)

**North American Range:** Western and southwestern United States, Mexico, and Central America

**Habitat:** Caves, trees, bridges, and attics

**Diet:** Moths and other insects

**FUN FACT**
Bracken Cave is near San Antonio, Texas. It is home to about 15 million Mexican free-tailed bats during the summer months. This is the largest known bat colony in the world.

Mexican free-tailed bats live in large colonies. They roost in caves, under bridges, and in attics. Some colonies contain millions of bats. A colony can eat 250 short tons (230 metric tons) of insects in one night. Mexican free-tailed bats migrate seasonally between the southern United States and Mexico.

Mating occurs during the spring, and females give birth to one pup a year. Pups roost in separate caves from their mothers. Mothers return to their pups to nurse them several times each day.

# POCKETED FREE-TAILED BAT

## *(NYCTINOMOPS FEMOROSACCUS)*

The pocketed free-tailed bat is small in size. It is named for a fold of skin behind its knees that forms a pocket. The bat's fur is brown, sometimes with red or gray tints. The bat has a wrinkled lip. Its ears connect at the middle of its forehead. Long hairs extend from its rear, likely to help the bat sense its surroundings.

### HOW TO SPOT

**Size:** Average wingspan of 13.4 to 14.6 inches (34 to 37 cm); 0.4 to 0.5 ounces (11.3 to 14.2 g)

**North American Range:** Southwestern United States to Mexico

**Habitat:** Semiarid deserts

**Diet:** Moths, wasps, beetles, and other flying insects

Pocketed free-tailed bats are relatively rare. They have a wide range. These bats usually roost along rocky ledges or in caves in colonies of about 100 individuals. Pocketed free-tailed bats can be noisy. They make a sharp, high-pitched call in flight and when leaving the roosting site. They flap their narrow wings quickly while flying. The bats may swoop down over water for a drink mid flight.

# VELVETY FREE-TAILED BAT

## *(MOLOSSUS MOLOSSUS)*

The velvety free-tailed bat is medium sized with long, narrow wings. Short, dense fur gives the bat its velvet-like appearance. Its fur is reddish brown to black. Its ears point forward and are joined together at the base. The bat has a dog-like face. Because of this, it is also called Pallas's mastiff bat after the mastiff dog breed.

While these bats can form groups as large as 50 to 300 individuals, they are known to roost in smaller groups, often less than 25 individuals. The bat is crepuscular. This means it is more active at dawn and dusk.

Velvety free-tailed bats hunt together. They use a technique called frequency hopping. They make two calls in quick succession that differ in pitch. The sound waves from the calls bounce back at slightly different times, allowing the bats to more accurately locate prey.

## HOW TO SPOT

**Size:** Wingspan of 10 to 12 inches (25.4 to 30.5 cm); 0.4 to 0.5 ounces (11.3 to 14.2 g)

**North American Range:** Florida Keys, Caribbean islands, and Central America

**Habitat:** Hardwood forests and human-made structures

**Diet:** Beetles, flies, ants, moths, and other flying insects

Pipistrelle bat

## ECHOLOCATION

Many bats use echolocation to navigate and find prey. They make high-pitched sounds that are too high for humans to hear. Sound waves bounce off the bats' surroundings. By listening to the echoes, bats can determine the distance, size, and even texture of nearby objects.

# WAGNER'S BONNETED BAT

## *(EUMOPS GLAUCINUS)*

Wagner's bonneted bat has black, brown, or gray fur. It is a medium-sized bat, and males are slightly larger than females. Wagner's bonneted bat is named for its wide ears, which look like a bonnet. The bat's narrow wings allow it to fly quickly for long periods of time. Wagner's bonneted bat has a musky odor, which may be used to mark territory.

### HOW TO SPOT

**Size:** Wingspan of 16 to 19 inches (40.6 to 48.3 cm); 1.1 to 1.6 ounces (31.2 to 45.4 g)

**North American Range:** Mexico, Cuba, Jamaica, and Central America

**Habitat:** Subtropical and tropical forests

**Diet:** Beetles, moths, and other flying insects

Tropical forests provide the ideal habitat for Wagner's bonneted bat.

Wagner's bonneted bat usually lives in tropical and subtropical forests. It shelters in tree canopies, sometimes taking over abandoned woodpecker nests. In urban areas it may roost along metal roofs. This bat is nocturnal. It becomes less active in cooler temperatures.

Wagner's bonneted bats live in small colonies that consist of a single male and several females. A male mates with multiple females. A female gives birth to one pup, which is weaned after five or six weeks.

# WESTERN MASTIFF BAT

## *(EUMOPS PEROTIS)*

The western mastiff bat is the largest bat in the United States, with a wingspan nearly 2 feet (0.6 m). Its large ears connect at the top of the skull and extend forward past the snout. This bat is also called the greater bonneted bat and the western bonneted bat. The western mastiff bat has brown or grayish-brown fur with white roots. A pouch-shaped gland on the bat's throat secretes an odor. This gland is more pronounced in male bats.

The western mastiff bat roosts in rocky crevices, cliff faces, and tall buildings. The bat feeds at night, foraging for insects in flight. It swoops down to drink from open water sources. As water sources shrink due to drought and other factors, the western mastiff bat population is declining in certain areas.

**FUN FACT**

**The western mastiff bat rarely returns to its roost at night. It may spend six to seven hours straight hunting for insects.**

## HOW TO SPOT

**Size:** Wingspan of 21 to 24 inches (53 to 61 cm); 2.1 to 2.5 ounces (59.5 to 70.9 g)

**North American Range:** Southwestern United States to Mexico

**Habitat:** Open, dry habitats with cliffs and rocky ledges

**Diet:** Flying insects, ants, and crickets

# GHOST-FACED BAT

## *(MORMOOPS MEGALOPHYLLA)*

Ghost-faced bats are medium-sized bats with fur that ranges from reddish brown to dark brown. These bats have faces that look flattened, with eyes almost within their ears. Their round ears curve around their foreheads. Ghost-faced bats have multiple folds of skin across their chins.

### HOW TO SPOT

**Size:** Wingspan of 14 to 15 inches (35.6 to 38.1 cm); 0.5 to 0.7 ounces (14.2 to 19.8 g)

**North American Range:** Southern Texas through Central America and Caribbean islands

**Habitat:** Warm climates, including desert scrublands, woodlands, and tropical rainforests

**Diet:** Moths and other large insects

**FUN FACT**
Scientists have found fossils of the ghost-faced bat throughout Central America. Some of these fossils date back to 20,000 years ago.

Ghost-faced bats live in colonies with as many as half a million individuals. These bats roost about 6 inches (15 cm) apart in caves and abandoned mines that are warm and humid. At night, ghost-faced bats leave their roosting sites in large groups to hunt for insects. They drink during flight by swooping down to a water source and extending their tongues into the water. Females give birth to one pup between April and June. Mothers and pups live separately from other bats in the warmest part of a cave.

# BIG-EARED WOOLLY BAT

## *(CHROTOPTERUS AURITUS)*

The big-eared woolly bat is named for its large, oval-shaped ears. This large bat has dark brown fur that becomes paler toward its bottom. Like other leaf-nosed bats, this bat has a long, leaf-like shape on its nose that is believed to help with echolocation. The bat has sharp teeth and is sometimes called the woolly false vampire bat. It has oval-shaped wings that each end in a long claw.

### HOW TO SPOT

**Size:** Average wingspan of 1.5 feet (0.5 m); 2.6 to 3.4 ounces (73.7 to 96.4 g)

**North American Range:** Southern Mexico to Central America

**Habitat:** Tropical forests near streams

**Diet:** Rodents, birds, smaller bats, insects, and fruits

### SEXUAL DIMORPHISM

Big-eared woolly bats show sexual dimorphism. This means that males and females of this species look noticeably different. Males have pronounced glands on their chests. These glands release an odor used for mating purposes. Some females have these glands too, but they do not produce an odor. Female big-eared woolly bats are larger than males, outweighing them by about 0.7 ounces (19.8 g).

These bats live in small colonies that usually contain fewer than ten individuals. Females give birth to one pup a year. The big-eared woolly bat uses echolocation to find moving prey. The bat wraps its wings around its prey and locks its wing claws together to trap the animal. It bites the creature's throat or head to kill it.

# CALIFORNIA LEAF-NOSED BAT

*(MACROTUS CALIFORNICUS)*

California leaf-nosed bats have gray to dark brown fur with paler underbellies. They are the only bats in the United States with large ears and a nose leaf. These bats have short, broad wings that allow them to fly without using much energy.

California leaf-nosed bats fly just above the ground to hunt insects. Good eyesight allows these bats to spot prey. A good sense of hearing means they can hear insects' footsteps.

**FUN FACT**

**California leaf-nosed bats are the only North American bats known to eat caterpillars. The bats grab the caterpillars off the ground while in flight.**

## HOW TO SPOT

**Size:** Wingspan of 13 to 14 inches (33 to 35.6 cm); 0.3 to 0.6 ounces (8 to 17 g)

**North American Range:** Southwestern United States to western Mexico

**Habitat:** Caves, abandoned mines, and rocky desert areas

**Diet:** Crickets, grasshoppers, caterpillars, other insects, and cactus fruits

These bats mate in the fall, and females give birth to one pup in late spring to early summer. They have a relatively long gestation period for bats, lasting about eight months. California leaf-nosed bats are born with a full coat of fur and developed ears and eyes.

# COMMON VAMPIRE BAT

## *(DESMODUS ROTUNDUS)*

Vampire bats have grayish-brown fur that is lighter on their bellies. The bats have pointed ears and no tail. Their long thumbs let them move quickly on the ground.

### A HELPFUL TRAIT

Vampire bats are often thought of as pests. The bats carry diseases, and infections due to vampire bat bites cause millions of dollars of loss to the cattle industry each year. But the anticlotting properties of the bat's saliva have led to important medical developments. The proteins have been used to develop medications that can prevent medical conditions such as strokes.

## HOW TO SPOT

**Size:** Wingspan of 14 to 16 inches (35.6 to 40.6 cm); 0.5 to 1.8 ounces (14.2 to 51 g)

**North American Range:** Mexico to Central America

**Habitat:** Caves, tree hollows, and human-made structures in tropical and subtropical climates

**Diet:** Blood from large mammals such as livestock

**Vampire bats are the only bat species capable of leaping from the ground into flight.**

Vampire bats consume blood. Their noses sense heat, helping the bats find their victims. The bats leap onto the victim, make an incision with their sharp teeth, and lap the blood with their tongues. While vampire bats do sometimes feed on humans, it is very rare. Vampire bats feed for about 30 minutes and may double their weight in this time.

A colony of vampire bats ranges from about 100 to 1,000 individuals. Female vampire bats groom their pups and each other. Bats regurgitate and share food with members of the colony who were unsuccessful with their hunt.

# FRINGE-LIPPED BAT

## *(TRACHOPS CIRRHOSUS)*

The fringe-lipped bat has coarse, woolly fur that ranges from brown to gray. It has a leaf nose with saw-like edges and long ears that are larger than its head. The bat hunts frogs and is sometimes called the frog-eating bat. It has wart-like bumps along its lips and chin. The bumps are thought to safeguard the bats from toxins on frog skin.

### HOW TO SPOT

**Size:** Wingspan data unavailable; 1.1 to 1.6 ounces (31.2 to 45.4 g)

**North American Range:** Southern Mexico to Central America

**Habitat:** Caves and moist forests

**Diet:** Frogs, insects, small vertebrates, and fruits

The bat flies in circles over open ponds, listening for the call of male frogs. It also uses echolocation to find frogs. When it detects prey, the bat swoops down and covers the area with its wings and tail membrane. Then it uses its mouth to find the prey. The bat secures the prey in its mouth before flying to a perch to eat.

Fringe-lipped bats live in small colonies, but they are social. Young bats observe mature bats to learn how to identify frog calls. These bats also communicate by scent.

# JAMAICAN FRUIT BAT

## *(ARTIBEUS JAMAICENSIS)*

The Jamaican fruit bat is heavy and has dark fur that ranges from black to brown or gray. It has a white stripe above and below each eye. The bat has bumps along its chin and a large nose leaf that looks like a third ear. Its large canine teeth help it bite into hard, unripe fruits.

**FUN FACT**

Individual Jamaican fruit bats do not have a strong odor. However, a colony of Jamaican fruit bats gives off a noticeable perfumed, soapy aroma.

## HOW TO SPOT

**Size:** Wingspan of 3.8 to 5.9 inches (9.7 to 15 cm); 1.4 to 2.1 ounces (39.7 to 59.5 g)

**North American Range:** Central Mexico through Central America, the Florida Keys, Puerto Rico, Jamaica, and the Virgin Islands

**Habitat:** Lowland rainforests, deciduous forests, and plantations

**Diet:** Figs, pollen, nectar, and tropical fruits

Hundreds of Jamaican fruit bats may eat from the same fruit tree in a night. Then the bats pass the seeds in their stool during flight, distributing them throughout their ecosystem.

The Jamaican fruit bat roosts in caves and hollow trees. It may also make tents out of leaves. A male lives with a small number of females and their young. The male protects the group from rival males. Jamaican fruit bats make a series of distress calls to warn one another of predators.

# LESSER LONG-NOSED BAT

## *(LEPTONYCTERIS YERBABUENAE)*

Lesser long-nosed bats are yellowish brown to gray in color. They have small ears and short tails. This bat has a nose leaf, though it is relatively small. The bat has a long, narrow snout and a tongue as long as its body. It also has a strong sense of smell. These are important features for gathering food. These bats may travel a total of 62 miles (100 km) each night searching for food.

**FUN FACT**

**Lesser long-nosed bats are important pollinators. They pollinate agave plants, saguaro cacti, and organ pipe cacti. These bats also help spread cactus seeds throughout their habitat.**

Lesser long-nosed bats live in large colonies. These groups may include hundreds of thousands of individuals. This helps keep the bats warm and lets young pups grow more quickly.

Due to habitat loss, the lesser long-nosed bat was once a threatened species. This means the bat's population was declining. But conservation measures allowed populations to recover. The species is no longer endangered.

## HOW TO SPOT

**Size:** Average wingspan of 10 inches (25.4 cm); 0.5 to 0.9 ounces (14.2 to 25.5 g)

**North American Range:** Southwestern United States to south-central Mexico

**Habitat:** Dry grasslands, desert scrublands, and dry tropical forests

**Diet:** Nectar from cacti

# MEXICAN LONG-NOSED BAT

*(LEPTONYCTERIS NIVALIS)*

The Mexican long-nosed bat looks like other nectar-drinking bats, but it has a long third finger. Its pale brown to gray fur is darker and fluffier as well. The bat has a triangular nose leaf.

## HOW TO SPOT

**Size:** Average wingspan of 14 inches (35.6 cm); 0.6 to 1.1 ounces (17 to 31.2 g)

**North American Range:** Southwestern United States, Mexico, Honduras, and Guatemala

**Habitat:** Woodlands and desert scrublands

**Diet:** Agave, cactus, and morning glory nectar and pollen; fruits; and insects

## FUN FACT

Mexican long-nosed bats and agave plants rely on each other for survival. The bats need these plants for food, and agave plants depend on the bats for pollination.

**Mexican long-nosed bats roost in a cave in Big Bend National Park in southwest Texas.**

The Mexican long-nosed bat lives at higher elevations than other nectar-drinking bats. These areas are colder, requiring the bats to use more energy to survive. The Mexican long-nosed bat has adapted to this environment. Its digestive system lets it absorb more energy from nectar than other species. This bat migrates to follow the seasonal blooms of agave plants.

Mexican long-nosed bats roost in caves and abandoned mines as well as along cliff faces. Caves protect the bats from hot desert temperatures. Colony sizes range from a few individuals to thousands of bats.

# MEXICAN LONG-TONGUED BAT

## *(CHOERONYCTERIS MEXICANA)*

The Mexican long-tongued bat is a medium-sized bat with a long, narrow snout that ends with a nose leaf. It has brown or gray fur and is lighter on its underside. The bat has small ears and a short, visible tail. Its tongue unfurls to a total length of more than 1 inch (2.5 cm), allowing it to drink from night-blooming flowers.

Mexican long-tongued bats migrate to follow seasonal blooms. Their range extends into the United States during the summer. They migrate south into Mexico and Central America for the winter.

Female bats give birth to one pup in the summer. Pups are born with fur that keeps them warm in cool mountain roosts. They can fly about two to three weeks after birth.

**FUN FACT**

Female Mexican long-nosed bats have been seen carrying their young in flight.

## HOW TO SPOT

**Size:** Wingspan of up to 14 inches (35.6 cm); average 0.9 ounces (25.5 g)

**North American Range:** Southwestern United States, Mexico, and Central America

**Habitat:** Desert canyons, scrublands, dry grasslands, and woodlands

**Diet:** Pollen, nectar, fruits, and insects

# SPECTRAL BAT *(VAMPYRUM SPECTRUM)*

With a wingspan of nearly 3 feet (0.9 m), the spectral bat is the largest bat in the Western Hemisphere. The spectral bat has short, fine reddish-brown fur. It has large ears and a large nose leaf. The bat has four sharp teeth on its upper and lower jaws, so it is sometimes called the great or greater false vampire bat. But it does not drink blood.

The spectral bat tracks prey by scent. It can catch flying prey and scoop prey from the forest floor. Then the bat wraps its wings around its prey and bites the head or neck.

Spectral bats are monogamous. A mated pair lives with and cares for their young together. The female usually stays with the pups while the male hunts for the family's food.

**FUN FACT**

**The spectral bat is the largest carnivorous bat in the world.**

## HOW TO SPOT

**Size:** Wingspan of 28 to 35 inches (71.1 to 88.9 cm); 6 to 6.3 ounces (170.1 to 178.6 g)

**North American Range:** Southern Mexico through Central America

**Habitat:** Moist, lowland forests near water

**Diet:** Birds, rodents, and other bats

# WRINKLE-FACED BAT

## *(CENTURIO SENEX)*

The wrinkle-faced bat has gray or brown fur and a white beard. It has a unique wing pattern. Sections of its wing membrane appear transparent, and other sections have a crosshatch pattern. The bat has a broad, flat face and large eyes. Its face is covered in wrinkles that are believed to help funnel fruit juices to its mouth. Males have additional skin folds that contain scent glands used to attracts mates.

### HOW TO SPOT

**Size:** Wingspan data unavailable; 0.5 to 1 ounce (14.2 to 28.4 g)

**North American Range:** Central America

**Habitat:** Forests

**Diet:** Overripe fruits, including mangoes and bananas

Wrinkle-faced bats roost in trees. They roost alone or in small groups of no more than a dozen bats. Males and females roost together only during breeding season. The bats roost with their wings pulled around them. Because their wings are translucent, the bats can still detect light and movement through their wings.

# ALLEN'S BIG-EARED BAT

## *(IDIONYCTERIS PHYLLOTIS)*

Allen's big-eared bat is named for its large ears, which are around 1 to 1.5 inches (2.5 to 3.8 cm) long. A lobe called a lappet extends from the forehead and sits in front of each ear. The bat's fur is black at the root and yellowish gray toward the tip. A patch of white fur marks the base of each ear.

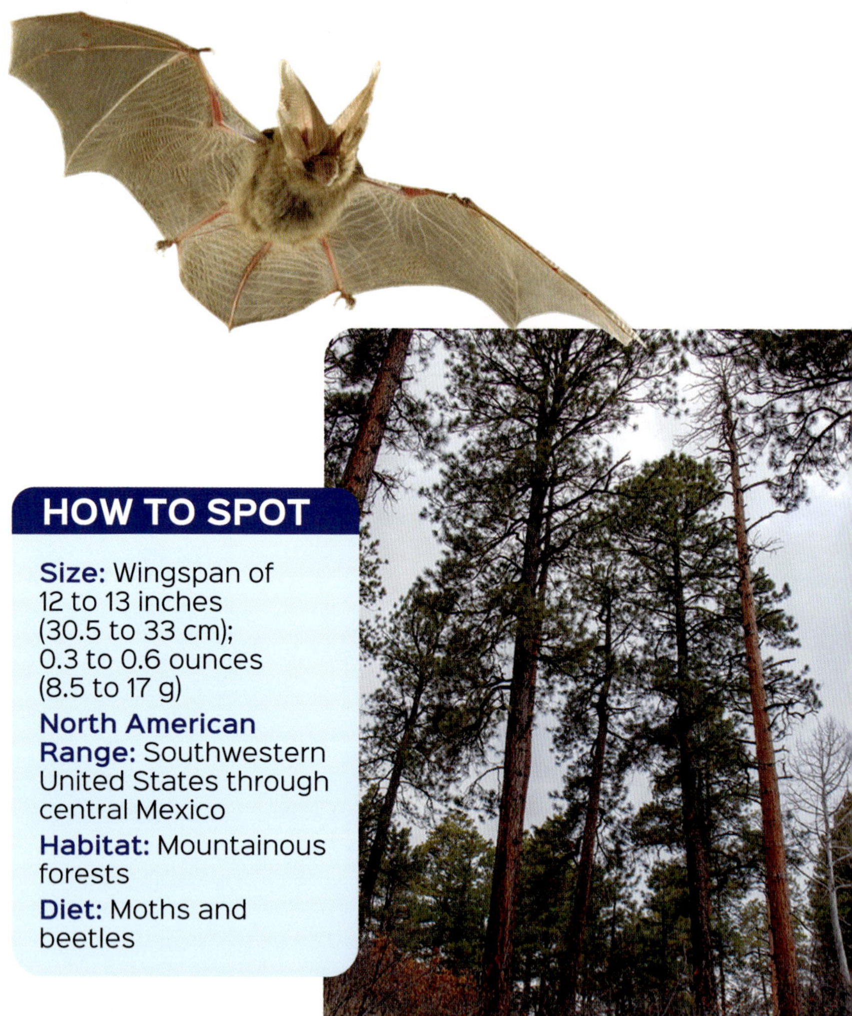

### HOW TO SPOT

**Size:** Wingspan of 12 to 13 inches (30.5 to 33 cm); 0.3 to 0.6 ounces (8.5 to 17 g)

**North American Range:** Southwestern United States through central Mexico

**Habitat:** Mountainous forests

**Diet:** Moths and beetles

Allen's big-eared bat is a fast, agile flyer that can hover in place. It uses echolocation to navigate and find prey. The bat hunts over open water, catching flying insects, including moths.

Allen's big-eared bat lives at elevations ranging from 3,000 to 10,000 feet (914 to 3,048 m). The bats depend on rocky crevices and ponderosa pine forests to roost and raise their young. These habitats have been shrinking, making Allen's big-eared bat one of the rarest bats in North America.

# ARIZONA MYOTIS *(MYOTIS OCCULTUS)*

The Arizona myotis is a small bat with glossy fur. The fur on its back is brown, while its underside is grayer in color. The ears, feet, and wings of the Arizona myotis range from light brown to black. Populations of Arizona myotises have slightly different head and skull shapes depending on the prey they eat, which varies by region.

## HOW TO SPOT

**Size:** Wingspan of 9.4 to 10 inches (23.9 to 25.4 cm); 0.25 to 0.3 ounces (7 to 8.5 g)

**North American Range:** Southwestern United States and Mexico

**Habitat:** Pine forests, deserts, and caves

**Diet:** Insects, including moths, ants, and beetles

Arizona myotises mate in the fall before hibernating. Sperm from the male bat is stored in the female's reproductive tract through the winter. The egg cell is fertilized when the female emerges from hibernation. Females give birth to a single pup in the summer. Pups are well developed at birth and are fully furred. They can fly on their own after four weeks.

## MYOTIS LIFESPAN

The Arizona myotis lives for six to seven years. One male captured in the wild was 31 years old. But many bats do not survive beyond their first winter. Bats must have a high fat reserve to hibernate throughout the winter months. Young, small bats hunt for insects later into the fall than older adults in order to maximize food intake.

# BIG BROWN BAT *(EPTESICUS FUSCUS)*

The big brown bat is a large bat with fur that ranges from pinkish tan to dark brown. Its fur has an oily appearance, and the fur on its belly is darker than the fur on its back. The bat's face, ears, wings, and tail membrane are black. The big brown bat has a large head with big eyes, fleshy lips, and sharp teeth.

## WHITE NOSE SYNDROME

White nose syndrome is a disease that devastates populations of cave-hibernating bats, including the big brown bat. The disease is caused by a fungus that grows as a white fuzz on the faces of bats. The first case of white nose syndrome was documented in New York in 2006. Since then, the disease has spread throughout North America and killed millions of bats. In extreme cases, 90 to 100 percent of a colony affected by white nose syndrome dies over the winter.

## HOW TO SPOT

**Size:** Wingspan of 12 to 16 inches (30.5 to 40.6 cm); 0.4 to 0.8 ounces (11.3 to 22.7 g)

**North American Range:** Canada through Central America

**Habitat:** Deciduous forests, meadows, deserts, and urban and suburban areas

**Diet:** Beetles and other flying insects

Big brown bats mate before hibernating in caves, mines, and buildings in the fall. Fertilization does not occur until the spring. After emerging from hibernation, big brown bats fly to summer foraging grounds. Female bats give birth to one or two pups in June or July. The bats have a high mortality rate during the first winter but can survive up to 19 years in the wild.

# CALIFORNIA MYOTIS

### *(MYOTIS CALIFORNICUS)*

The California myotis is one of the smallest bats in North America. In general the bat has a dull coloration that ranges from rusty to dark brown. Bats living in desert habitats may appear yellowish, and those living at higher elevations tend to be darker in color than those at lower elevations. The ears, wings, and tail membrane of the California myotis are black. California myotises have rounded wing tips, which allow for slow, acrobatic flight.

## HOW TO SPOT

**Size:** Wingspan of 9 to 10 inches (22.9 to 25.4 cm); 0.1 to 0.2 ounces (2.8 to 5.7 g)

**North American Range:** Western North America from southern Alaska to Guatemala

**Habitat:** Desert scrublands and woodlands

**Diet:** Flies, moths, beetles, and other flying insects

The California myotis roosts alone or in small groups. It roosts in caves, mines, and buildings and under the bark of certain types of trees, such as the ponderosa pine. This bat switches roosts regularly to avoid predators such as snakes and raccoons. After switching roosts, California myotises rarely return to an old roosting site.

# CANYON BAT

## *(PARASTRELLUS HESPERUS)*

Canyon bats are also called western pipistrelle bats. They are small with gray fur. They have black, leathery faces and ears. Their wing membranes are also black. Canyon bats can be identified by their ear shape compared with other bats in their range. The tragus is short and blunt.

**FUN FACT**

Many bats give birth to only one pup each year. But canyon bats usually give birth to twins.

## HOW TO SPOT

**Size:** Wingspan of 7 to 9 inches (17.8 to 22.9 cm); 0.1 to 0.2 ounces (2.8 to 5.7 g)

**North American Range:** Western United States to Mexico

**Habitat:** Deserts, woodlands, and shrublands

**Diet:** Small swarming insects, such as moths, mosquitoes, and fruit flies

Canyon bats are named for the canyon habitats and rocky cliffs where they live. The bats often roost in caves, abandoned mines, and rodent burrows. These bats hibernate during the winter months, but they come out of their roosts during warm winter days to look for food.

Canyon bats are nocturnal. During a single night of feeding, they can eat 20 percent of their body weight in insects. Flying through a swarm allows them to eat a large number of insects fairly quickly.

# CAVE MYOTIS *(MYOTIS VELIFER)*

The cave myotis is a medium-sized bat with dark brown or black fur. The fur on its belly is paler than the fur on its back, and the bat has a bare patch of skin on its back between the shoulder blades. This bat has small eyes and pointy ears.

**FUN FACT**

**The cave myotis is larger than other bats in the *Myotis* genus. Because of its large size, it is a strong flier and has a wider foraging range than similar species.**

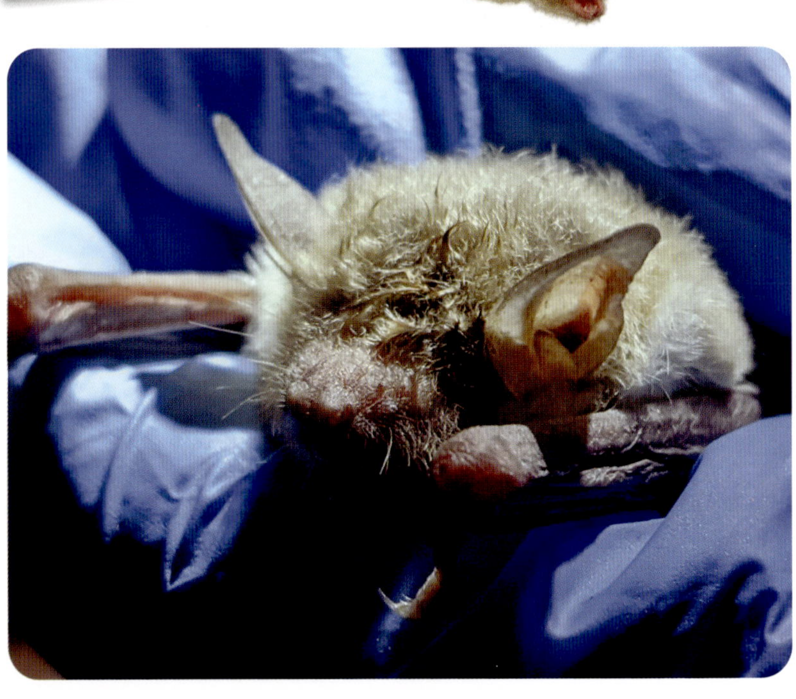

The cave myotis roosts in caves and human-made structures such as mines, buildings, and bridges. The bat also roosts in swallow nests. If a site is disturbed by human activity, the cave myotis will abandon its roost.

Cave myotises gather in large colonies that are usually around 5,000 individuals, but some are much larger, including approximately 15,000 bats. Clustering tightly together provides warmth during hibernation in the winter months. This also protects newborn bats, which roost alongside their mothers.

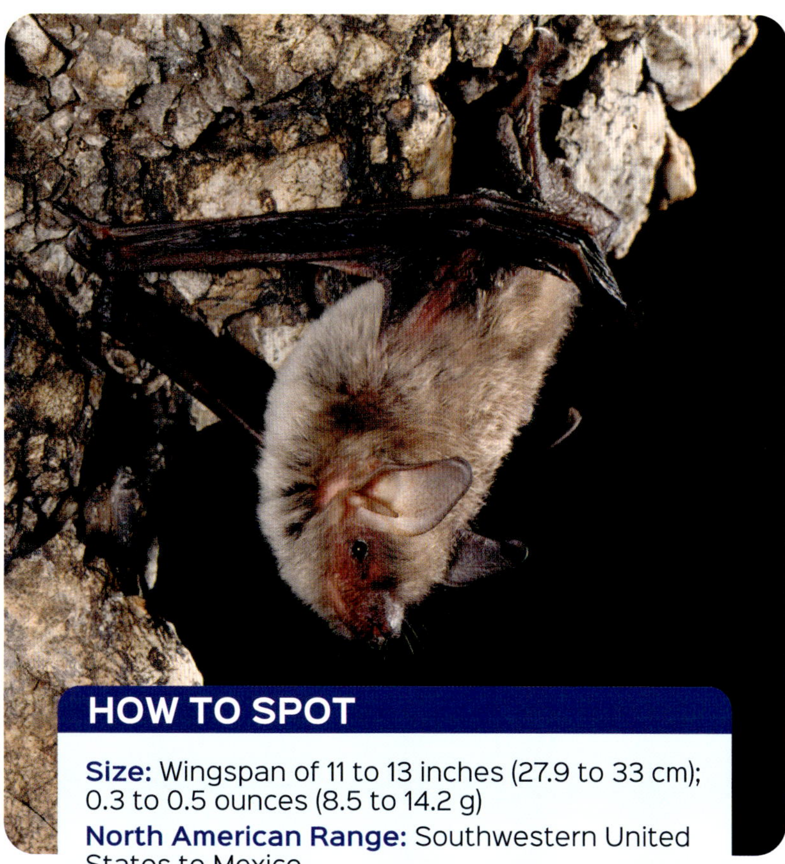

## HOW TO SPOT

**Size:** Wingspan of 11 to 13 inches (27.9 to 33 cm); 0.3 to 0.5 ounces (8.5 to 14.2 g)

**North American Range:** Southwestern United States to Mexico

**Habitat:** Caves and mines at low elevations

**Diet:** Moths, beetles, and weevils

# EASTERN RED BAT

## *(LASIURUS BOREALIS)*

The eastern red bat has reddish-orange fur with white tips, giving the bat a frosty appearance. Male bats are more brightly colored than females, which appear more gray. The eastern red bat has long, silky fur all over that grows along its tail membrane as well.

### HOW TO SPOT

**Size:** Wingspan of about 13 inches (33 cm); 0.3 to 0.5 ounces (8.5 to 14.2 g)

**North American Range:** Southern Canada, eastern United States, and northeastern Mexico

**Habitat:** Forests, pastures, and croplands

**Diet:** Moths, beetles, and other insects

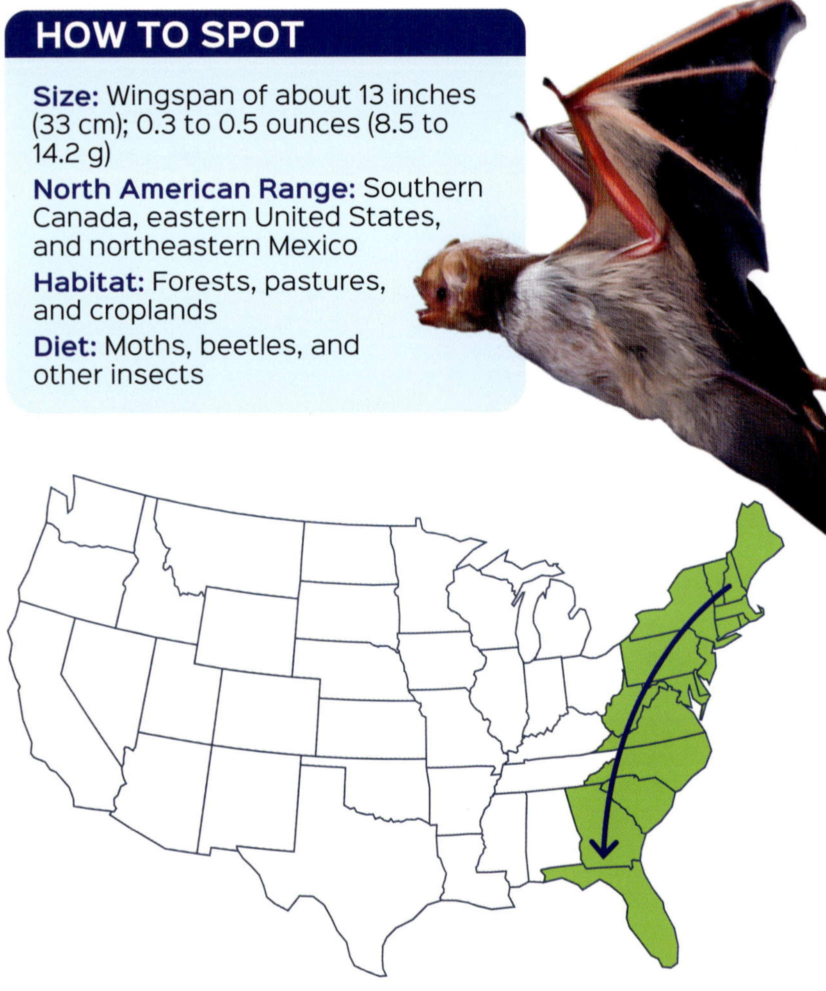

**Eastern red bats migrate along the Atlantic flyway.**

Most eastern red bats migrate to warmer climates during the fall. They follow the migration route of many bird species along the Atlantic coast. Some populations do not migrate. Instead, they hibernate in trees, wrapping their furred tail membrane around them like a blanket for warmth.

Unlike many bat species, the eastern red bat gives birth to multiple pups each year. An average litter includes three pups but may have as many as five pups. The female eastern red bat has two pairs of teats, allowing up to four pups to drink milk at once.

# EASTERN SMALL-FOOTED MYOTIS *(MYOTIS LEIBII)*

The eastern small-footed myotis has glossy brown fur with a golden sheen. It has a black face, making the bat look as if it is wearing a mask. The bat's ears and wings are also black. Its very small feet measure less than 0.8 inches (2 cm) long.

The eastern small-footed myotis usually roosts in caves, in mines, and along rocky ledges. It may roost in buildings and under bridges as well. The bat does not migrate, but it changes roosts daily. It returns to the same hibernation site each year. The bat's small size allows it to squeeze into rocky crevices where it hibernates lying down.

The bat flies slow and low, fluttering about 3 to 9 feet (0.9 to 2.7 m) above the ground. It flies over water to catch flying insects and can eat its fill for the day in an hour.

## HOW TO SPOT

**Size:** Wingspan of 8.3 to 10 inches (21 to 25.4 cm); 0.12 to 0.2 ounces (3.4 to 5.7 g)

**North American Range:** Southeastern Canada and northeastern United States

**Habitat:** Near forests in caves, mines, and other rocky areas

**Diet:** Flies, moths, other insects, and spiders

The eastern small-footed myotis hibernates in narrow rock crevices.

# EVENING BAT *(NYCTICEIUS HUMERALIS)*

The evening bat is small with black wings and ears. Its dark brown fur is darker at the roots and grayer toward the tips. It has a rounded tragus in front of its ears. The evening bat looks similar to the big brown bat and has a dog-like muzzle, but the evening bat is noticeably smaller.

## HOW TO SPOT

**Size:** Wingspan of 10 to 11 inches (25.4 to 27.9 cm); 0.2 to 0.5 ounces (5.7 to 14.2 g)

**North American Range:** Central and southeastern United States to northern Mexico

**Habitat:** Forests and wetlands

**Diet:** Beetles, flies, and moths

Evening bats live in forests, roosting beneath loose bark and in tree crevices. Deforestation has forced evening bats to sometimes roost in buildings. The bats find prey using echolocation. A colony of 300 evening bats was estimated to eat approximately 6.3 million insects each summer. These bats migrate to warmer climates in the winter.

In summer, females form maternity colonies, which can include several hundred individuals. They give birth to two or three pups each year. Pups are born blind and hairless but are able to fly after about three weeks.

## TRACKING BATS

Scientists use a variety of methods to study bats. They may use a mist net, a thin net strung between two poles, to capture bats. They record the bat's size and weight, observe the bat for disease, and sometimes take a fur sample. Scientists may also band the bats, attaching a tracking device to the animal to study its activity patterns. One evening bat migrated 340 miles (550 km) from where it was banded.

# FISH-EATING BAT *(MYOTIS VIVESI)*

The fish-eating bat is the largest member of the *Myotis* genus in the Western Hemisphere. Its fur ranges from pale tan to brown, though the roots may appear gray. The bat's large wings allow it to fly without using much energy, but they can make it difficult to move through tight spaces.

**FUN FACT**
The fish-eating bat sometimes shelters in empty turtle shells.

The fish-eating bat hunts the waters of the Sea of Cortez.

## HOW TO SPOT

**Size:** Wingspan data unavailable; about 0.9 ounces (25.5 g)

**North American Range:** Along Mexico's Baja California peninsula

**Habitat:** Caves and rocky coastal areas

**Diet:** Crustaceans, fish such as lanternfish, and insects

The bat's large feet make up nearly 15 percent of its body length. Its feet end in long claws. This is one of two bats in North America that hunts sea animals. It skims its claws along the surface of the water to hook prey. The bat may eat its meal in flight or fly to a perch to eat. Invasive predators, habitat loss, and climate change have made the fish-eating bat a vulnerable species. This means it is at high risk of becoming endangered.

# FRINGED MYOTIS

## *(MYOTIS THYSANODES)*

The fringed myotis is named for the stiff, wire-like hairs extending from its tail membrane. Fur on the bat's back ranges from yellowish brown to dark olive. Some northern populations have fur that is lighter along their bellies. This bat has long ears that are black or brown.

The fringed myotis roosts in trees, caves, and buildings, usually close to sources of water. The bats often form colonies of 10 to 100 bats. Larger colonies may include thousands of individuals, but this is rare. The bats use echolocation to search for insects in the hours after sunset.

Female fringed myotises form maternity colonies around mid-May. They give birth to one pup in the early summer. After pups are born, some females remain in the colony to nurse pups while others go forage for insects.

## HOW TO SPOT

**Size:** Wingspan of 10 to 12 inches (25.4 to 30.5 cm); 0.2 to 0.3 ounces (5.7 to 8.5 g)

**North American Range:** Southwestern Canada, western United States, and Mexico

**Habitat:** Desert scrublands, evergreen forests, and oak woodlands

**Diet:** Beetles, moths, crickets, and other insects

In Oregon, leafhoppers make up a large part of the fringed myotis's diet.

# GRAY BAT *(MYOTIS GRISESCENS)*

The gray bat has grayish-brown fur that appears closer to a rusty brown in the summer. Its ears and wings range from gray to black. A gray bat's wing membrane attaches to its ankles. In many other bat species, wing membranes attach to the base of the first toe.

## HOW TO SPOT

**Size:** Wingspan of 10 to 11 inches (25.4 to 27.9 cm); 0.3 to 0.6 ounces (8.5 to 17 g)

**North American Range:** Southeastern United States

**Habitat:** Caves near sources of fresh water

**Diet:** Moths, flies, caddisflies, stoneflies, mayflies, beetles, weevils, and other insects

The gray bat uses echolocation to forage for insects over waterways. It eats during flight. During the summer, the bat prefers to eat Asiatic oak weevils, an invasive species.

Gray bats roost only in deep, tall caves that trap cold air. These sites are very rare. It is estimated that 98 percent of gray bats roost in 15 known hibernation sites across their range. Polluted waterways have affected gray bats, which were added to the endangered species list in 1976.

# HOARY BAT *(LASIURUS CINEREUS)*

The hoary bat is a widespread but uncommon bat. The bat has long, soft hair that is dark brown or black at the roots. The fur becomes white at the tips, giving the bat a cobwebbed appearance. The hoary bat also has a yellowish-cream collar around its face. This coloring makes it look like a dead leaf hanging from a tree branch.

## WIND TURBINES

Hoary bats are one of the bat species most heavily affected by wind turbines. These creatures sometimes collide with wind turbines during flight. It is estimated that 76,000 to 152,000 hoary bats are killed due to wind turbine collisions each year. Researchers are looking for ways to improve the safety of wind turbines for wildlife. For example, a wind turbine may make a sound to deter bats from flying too close.

## HOW TO SPOT

**Size:** Average wingspan of 17 inches (43.2 cm); 0.7 to 1.2 ounces (19.8 to 34 g)

**North American Range:** Canada through Central America

**Habitat:** Forest edges

**Diet:** Moths and other insects

**FUN FACT**

The hoary bat's long, narrow wings allow it to fly at speeds of up to 13 miles per hour (21 kmh).

During the winter months, this bat migrates to warmer habitats. It migrates in groups but roosts alone in old, mature trees. These bats change roosts regularly.

Hoary bats mate in the fall just before migrating. However, fertilization is delayed until the following spring. Females give birth while hanging upside down in a roosting site. They often have twins.

# INDIANA BAT *(MYOTIS SODALIS)*

The Indiana bat is a medium-sized bat with chestnut brown to dark gray fur on its back and lighter fur on its belly. The bat's ears and wings are also a dull gray color. This bat has small, delicate feet.

The Indiana bat uses echolocation to find prey during warm months. When temperatures begin to drop, Indiana bats swarm together in front of caves to mate before hibernating. They look for deep, tall caves or mines with temperatures above freezing but below 50 degrees Fahrenheit (10°C).

Fertilization happens after the Indiana bat emerges from hibernation. A single pup is born in midsummer and is able to fly about a month later. An Indiana bat will usually live about five or six years, but some individuals have lived more than 20 years. These bats are federally protected.

## HOW TO SPOT

**Size:** Wingspan of 9.4 to 11 inches (23.9 to 27.9 cm); 0.2 to 0.4 ounces (5.7 to 11.3 g)

**North American Range:** Central and northeastern United States

**Habitat:** Caves and forests

**Diet:** Insects

## FUN FACT

The Indiana bat is also called the social myotis. This is because they are highly social and like to cluster together.

# KEEN'S MYOTIS *(MYOTIS KEENII)*

The Keen's myotis has brown fur with dark patches on its shoulders and lighter fur on its belly. The bat has long ears and slim, pointed tragi. Its ears, wings, and tail membrane are dark brown or black. The bat's tail membrane is fringed with small hairs. Keen's myotis has short, broad wings that help it turn quickly in flight.

## HOW TO SPOT

**Size:** Wingspan of 8.3 to 10 inches (21 to 25.4 cm); 0.14 to 0.3 ounces (4 to 8.5 g)

**North American Range:** Alaska, British Columbia, and Washington

**Habitat:** Old-growth forests along the Pacific coast

**Diet:** Insects and spiders

**FUN FACT**
**One colony of Keen's myotises roosts in rock cracks that are heated by a hot spring on the Queen Charlotte Islands in British Columbia, Canada.**

The Keen's myotis prefers a mild climate in forests with large, old trees where it primarily roosts in tree cavities. However, the bats may also roost in rock crevices, small caves, and buildings. They hunt at night, flying slowly to capture insects in their path.

In late fall and winter, Keen's myotises look for caves, where they swarm and mate before hibernating. They emerge from hibernation in the spring. Females form maternity colonies of 30 to 40 individuals.

# LITTLE BROWN BAT

## *(MYOTIS LUCIFUGUS)*

The little brown bat has glossy brown fur with an almost metallic sheen. The bat's wing and tail membranes are dark brown or black and also have a glossy appearance. The fur on its back is darker at the base and yellowish or olive brown at the tips. This bat has small ears and large feet.

**FUN FACT**

A single little brown bat can eat as many as 1,200 insects in a single hour.

The little brown bat roosts in trees. It hunts for insects over bodies of fresh water. The bat looks for food around dusk and later in the night.

It is estimated that populations of little brown bats have diminished by 90 percent due to white nose syndrome. Colonies of thousands of little brown bats hibernate in warm, humid caves. The humidity and their large numbers cause the disease to spread quickly among the bats.

## HOW TO SPOT

**Size:** Wingspan of 8.7 to 11 inches (22.1 to 27.9 cm); 0.18 to 0.5 ounces (5.1 to 14.2 g)

**North American Range:** Alaska, Canada, and northern United States

**Habitat:** Mountains, forests, caves, meadows, and urban areas

**Diet:** Insects

# LONG-EARED MYOTIS

## *(MYOTIS EVOTIS)*

The long-eared myotis is named for its large, hairless ears, which are about 0.8 inches (2 cm) long. Its ears and wings are dark but not black. The bat has silky, dark brown fur with darker patches on its shoulders.

### HOW TO SPOT

**Size:** Wingspan of 8.3 to 10 inches (21 to 25.4 cm); 0.2 to 0.3 ounces (5.7 to 8.5 g)

**North American Range:** Pacific coast from southeastern Alaska to Mexico's Baja California peninsula

**Habitat:** Coastal forests

**Diet:** Moths, flies, and spiders

The long-eared myotis lives in forests, where it roosts in tree crevices and stumps. The bat flies slowly but can turn quickly around trees. It hunts at night, catching its prey in flight or grabbing insects from plants and rocks.

The long-eared myotis mates before hibernating in caves or mines during the winter. Fertilization occurs after it emerges from hibernation in the spring. Pregnant females form maternity colonies with as many as 30 individuals. They each give birth to a single pup in the late spring or early summer. Pups are able to fly after about a month.

# LONG-LEGGED MYOTIS

## *(MYOTIS VOLANS)*

The long-legged myotis has dark fur with a reddish tint. The dark fur on its belly partially covers the underside of the bat's wing membrane. The bat's wings and its small, rounded ears are dark. The tibia bones in its legs are long, and its feet are small.

The long-legged myotis roosts in tree and rock crevices, caves, mines, and buildings. It prefers to roost along forest edges that receive a lot of sunlight. Reproducing females are especially dependent on old trees. They roost under loose bark, which most commonly occurs in trees that are more than 100 years old.

During the winter, males and females gather in caves to mate before hibernating. Females give birth to a single pup in the summer. The long-legged myotis can live up to 21 years.

### HOW TO SPOT

**Size:** Wingspan of 9.4 to 11 inches (23.9 to 27.9 cm); 0.2 to 0.4 ounces (5.7 to 11.3 g)

**North American Range:** Western North America from southeastern Alaska to central Mexico

**Habitat:** Old-growth coniferous forests

**Diet:** Soft-bodied insects

### FUN FACT

Many long-legged myotises return to the same hibernation site each winter.

The long-legged myotis roosts in pine trees.

# NORTHERN LONG-EARED MYOTIS *(MYOTIS SEPTENTRIONALIS)*

The northern long-eared myotis is characterized by its long, rounded ears. The bat has a slightly longer tail and larger wings than other *Myotis* species of a similar size. It has dark brown fur along its back and pale brown fur on its belly.

During the summer these bats roost under loose bark and in tree crevices. They switch roosts as often as every two days. Northern long-eared myotises are nocturnal and use echolocation to find prey. They tend to follow forest edges, because these areas are rich with insects and the trees offer the bats some protection as they feed. Northern long-eared myotises usually return to the same caves and mines to hibernate each winter. They live for an average of eight to ten years in the wild.

## HOW TO SPOT

**Size:** Wingspan of 9 to 10 inches (22.9 to 25.4 cm); 0.2 to 0.3 ounces (5.7 to 8.5 g)

**North American Range:** Canada and eastern United States

**Habitat:** Forests

**Diet:** Insects and spiders

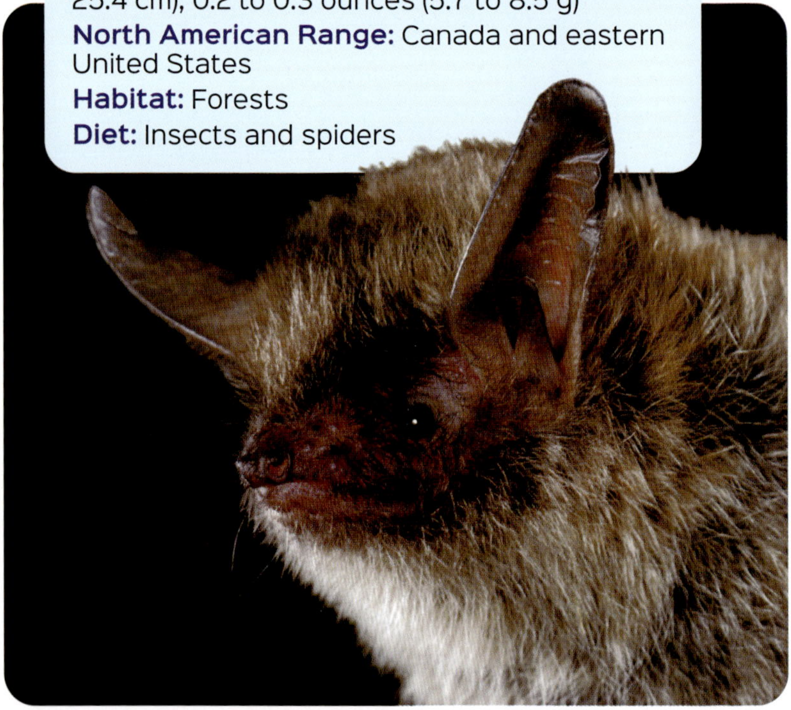

## SNEAKY HUNTERS

Northern long-eared myotises eat moths. Some moths have ears and can hear the echolocation calls of certain bats, which gives them a chance to avoid their predators. But northern long-eared myotises make high-pitched calls. The sounds are too high for moths to hear, allowing the bats to sneak up on them.

# NORTHERN YELLOW BAT

## *(LASIURUS INTERMEDIUS)*

The northern yellow bat ranges from yellowish orange to yellowish brown. It roosts among dead palm leaves, so its color serves as camouflage. The fur on its back is long and glossy. The upper half of the bat's tail membrane is furred. The bat has short, rounded ears.

### HOW TO SPOT

**Size:** Wingspan of 14 to 16 inches (35.6 to 40.6 cm); 0.6 to 0.8 ounces (17 to 22.7 g)

**North American Range:** Southeastern United States to eastern and southern Mexico

**Habitat:** Marine coasts

**Diet:** Mosquitoes, flies, beetles, and other insects

As many as 100 bats gather over grassy areas to hunt. Northern yellow bats do not hibernate. But they may become less active during long cold periods.

The northern yellow bat is rare, but it is common in some parts of its range, such as Florida. These bats form clusters when a female is raising her young. Females give birth to a litter of about three pups. Removal of roosting sites, such as dead palm fronds, threatens this species. Pesticides also affect populations, as the bats will move to areas where there is more prey.

# PALLID BAT *(ANTROZOUS PALLIDUS)*

The pallid bat is a large bat. It has cream-colored to yellowish-brown fur on its back and white fur on its belly. The bat has large ears, and its eyes are bigger than those of most North American bat species. The small, wart-like glands on its face give off a foul odor that is thought to be a way to drive away predators.

The pallid bat crawls on the ground to catch insects. The bat also eats scorpions. It is resistant to scorpion venom. After capturing a meal, the bat flies to a roost to eat. The pallid bat roosts in caves, trees, or buildings. It hibernates deep within caves or canyon crevices, where temperatures are consistent. Colonies usually have at least 20 individuals.

**FUN FACT**

**The large ears of the pallid bat are so sensitive that it can hear its prey's footsteps as the bat flies above the ground.**

## HOW TO SPOT

**Size:** Wingspan of 15 to 16 inches (38.1 to 40.6 cm); 0.6 to 1 ounce (17 to 28.4 g)

**North American Range:** Extreme southwestern Canada, western United States, Mexico, and Cuba

**Habitat:** Deserts and rocky ledges

**Diet:** Crickets, centipedes, other ground-dwelling insects, scorpions, lizards, and mice

# RAFINESQUE'S BIG-EARED BAT

## *(CORYNORHINUS RAFINESQUII)*

Rafinesque's big-eared bat has large ears that measure about 1.2 inches (3 cm) long. The tragus in front of each ear is long and pointed. The bat has dull, brownish-gray fur, though some may have a slight reddish tint. Long hairs extend beyond its claws, and it has glands on its snout. The purpose of the glands is unknown, but young bats do give off an odor.

### HOW TO SPOT

**Size:** Wingspan of 10 to 12 inches (25.4 to 30.5 cm); 0.3 to 0.5 ounces (8.5 to 14.2 g)

**North American Range:** Southeastern United States

**Habitat:** Woodlands and cypress swamps

**Diet:** Moths and other insects

**FUN FACT**
Rafinesque's big-eared bat can curl its large ears, making them look like the coiled horns of a ram. The bat does this while hibernating to prevent losing moisture through its ears.

Rafinesque's big-eared bat is a slow but agile flier that becomes active late at night. It catches insects in flight. The bat roosts in cypress swamps, forests, caves, and buildings. Rafinesque's big-eared bat hibernates near its hunting grounds in caves and abandoned mines. It mates before hibernating, and fertilization is delayed until spring. Females give birth to one pup in the summer. Mothers recognize their pups by scent. Due to habitat loss, the bat has been listed as threatened since 1977.

# SEMINOLE BAT *(LASIURUS SEMINOLUS)*

Seminole bats have reddish-brown or mahogany fur on their backs with paler fur on their bellies. They have a furry tail membrane, and fur also grows along the underside of the bats' wings. The bats have patches of white fur on their wrists and shoulders.

**FUN FACT**

Seminole bats are resourceful hunters. They sometimes forage for insects near streetlights because the light attracts their prey.

## HOW TO SPOT

**Size:** Average wingspan of about 12 inches (30.5 cm); 0.3 to 0.5 ounces (8.5 to 14.2 g)

**North American Range:** Southeastern United States

**Habitat:** Deciduous forests

**Diet:** Flies, beetles, crickets, and other insects

Seminole bats roost alone or with their young in forests with Spanish moss. They prefer to be shaded from the sun. Roost sites are usually 3.3 to 16 feet (1 to 5 m) above the ground.

Seminole bats do not hibernate, but they do become less active in cooler temperatures. They leave their roosts to forage only when temperatures are above 68 degrees Fahrenheit (20°C). In the late spring, Seminole bats give birth to as many as four pups. They often have twins.

# SILVER-HAIRED BAT

## *(LASIONYCTERIS NOCTIVAGANS)*

The silver-haired bat has fur that is black at the roots and whitish or silverish at the tips. This bat has dark brown to black wings. It has small, rounded ears and a slightly upturned snout.

**FUN FACT**

**When a silver-haired bat gives birth, she uses her tail membrane as a basket to catch her newborn pups.**

The silver-haired bat lives in forests and roosts in trees. Dead and dying trees are important roost sites, as the bat commonly roosts in tree crevices and under loose bark. Removal of dead trees to limit wildfires has a negative impact on the silver-haired bat.

In the winter, the silver-haired bat migrates south to hibernate in tree roosts, though species in the northern part of the range may shelter in cave entrances. Silver-haired bats mate before hibernation. Females store sperm until the spring. They give birth to two pups in late June or early July.

## HOW TO SPOT

**Size:** Wingspan of 11 to 12 inches (27.9 to 30.5 cm); 0.3 to 0.4 ounces (8.5 to 11.3 g)

**North American Range:** Southern Canada, United States, and northeastern Mexico

**Habitat:** Forests near fresh water

**Diet:** Insects

# SOUTHEASTERN MYOTIS

## *(MYOTIS AUSTRORIPARIUS)*

The southeastern myotis has short, thick fur that looks like wool. Its fur is dark gray or black at the base and whitish at the tips. The bat sheds its fur in late summer, revealing darker fur. The southeastern myotis has long toe hairs that extend past its claws.

The southeastern myotis roosts in tree hollows, caves, mines, and buildings. It prefers to roost near fresh water. The bat flies close to the water and uses echolocation to catch insects.

During the summer, females form large maternity colonies of as many as 100,000 bats. They look for nursery roosts that are warm and well insulated. Females give birth to two pups in late spring. Northern populations hibernate during the winter. Southern populations reduce their foraging activities but still emerge to hunt on warm winter nights.

## HOW TO SPOT

**Size:** Wingspan of 9.4 to 11 inches (23.9 to 27.9 cm); 0.2 to 0.3 ounces (5.7 to 8.5 g)

**North American Range:** Southeastern United States

**Habitat:** Woodlands near streams and lakes

**Diet:** Midges, mosquitoes, and aquatic insects

### FUN FACT

Though the southeastern myotis is born blind, deaf, and hairless, it can fly after five to six weeks.

# SOUTHERN YELLOW BAT

## *(LASIURUS EGA)*

Southern yellow bats are named for their dull, yellow fur. The fur extends down to the tail membrane. The bats have rounded ears.

Southern yellow bats live in woodlands in warm climates. They migrate toward the equator for the winter months. This means that North American populations migrate south, and some South American populations migrate north.

### HOW TO SPOT

**Size:** Average wingspan of 14 inches (35.6 cm); 0.4 to 0.6 ounces (11.3 to 17 g)

**North American Range:** Southwestern United States, Mexico, and Central America

**Habitat:** Forests

**Diet:** Insects

Southern yellow bats are typically solitary in nature. They gather in groups during migration. Females may form small maternity colonies when raising young. They have an average litter size of two to three pups.

Water sources are important foraging grounds for the southern yellow bat. At night the bat emerges to hunt for insects. It uses its tail membrane as a pouch to carry prey to its daytime roosts, where it feeds.

# SOUTHWESTERN MYOTIS

## *(MYOTIS AURICULUS)*

The southwestern myotis has dull, brown fur and long, brown ears. The flap of skin in front of each ear is narrow and pointed. The bat's wings are brown.

The southwestern myotis lives in dry climates near water sources, which provide hydration and a place to hunt. Females usually hunt for insects near water. They form small maternity colonies of about 30 individuals.

Southwestern myotises roost in dead ponderosa pines and woodpecker cavities. They also roost in buildings, mines, and caves. Little is known about the bats' hibernation roosts. However, researchers believe that the bats hibernate along rocky cliff faces, which are abundant throughout their habitat. The southwestern myotis is an important species in limiting pests that harm crops.

Colonies of southwestern myotises roost in the Chiricahua Mountains of southeastern Arizona.

## HOW TO SPOT

**Size:** Average wingspan of 11 inches (27.9 cm); 0.2 to 0.3 ounces (5.7 to 8.5 g)

**North American Range:** Southwestern United States and northern Mexico

**Habitat:** Dry woodlands and desert scrublands

**Diet:** Moths and other insects

# SPOTTED BAT *(EUDERMA MACULATUM)*

The spotted bat is a rare bat with a striking appearance. It has silky black fur on its back with white patches on its shoulders and rear. The fur on its belly is white. This bat has large, translucent ears that curl when the bat is resting. But when the bat is active, the ears unfurl to their full length of about 1.9 inches (4.7 cm). The spotted bat's ears and wings have a pinkish hue. Its face is black.

## HOW TO SPOT

**Size:** Average wingspan of 14 inches (35.6 cm); 0.6 to 0.7 ounces (17 to 19.8 g)

**North American Range:** Southwestern Canada, western United States, and northwestern Mexico

**Habitat:** Desert scrublands and open forests

**Diet:** Moths and other insects

**Spotted bats eat moths in the Noctuidae family. They tear off the wings before eating the bodies.**

The bat lives near sources of water and is territorial. It makes warning calls and flies at other spotted bats that enter its territory. The bat hunts at night and feeds primarily on moths, eating only the fleshy bodies. Newborn pups lack the spotted markings of adults. Their ears are also small. Females give birth to one pup in June.

# TOWNSEND'S BIG-EARED BAT

## *(CORYNORHINUS TOWNSENDII)*

Townsend's big-eared bat has fur that ranges from gray to brown and is darker at the roots than at the tips. The bat's large ears are about 1 inch (2.5 cm) long and connected at the base. Townsend's big-eared bat has a short snout with noticeable scent glands on either side of its nostrils. These glands are believed to produce odors when the bat is ready to mate.

The bat's large wings allow it to hover in place, making it possible for it to grab insects from plants. Townsend's big-eared bat roosts and hibernates in caves and mines, preferring open spaces rather than rock crevices. It hibernates in small colonies of males and females. During the spring, females form separate maternity colonies of about 100 adult bats. Disturbances during hibernation are stressful and can be deadly for the bat.

**FUN FACT**

Moths make up about 90 percent of the Townsend's big-eared bat's diet.

## HOW TO SPOT

**Size:** Wingspan of 12 to 13 inches (30.5 to 33 cm); 0.2 to 0.5 ounces (5.7 to 14.2 g)

**North American Range:** Southwestern Canada, western United States, regions of the Ozark and Appalachian Mountains, and Mexico

**Habitat:** Forests, deserts, prairies, and coasts

**Diet:** Moths and other insects

# TRICOLORED BAT

## *(PERIMYOTIS SUBFLAVUS)*

The tricolored bat is named for its fur pattern. The fur on the bat's back looks yellowish or grayish brown, but the hairs have a tricolored banding pattern. The roots and tips of its fur are dark, and the midsection is lighter in color. The bat's ears and wings are pale and slightly pink. Young tricolored bats are usually darker than adults.

During the spring and summer, the tricolored bat roosts in trees. It prefers trees with Spanish moss and beard lichen. This type of lichen produces an acid that may help keep away parasites and bacteria.

Tricolored bats in the north hibernate in caves. Some populations of tricolored bats migrate south. Bats that live in the south reduce their activity in cooler months but emerge during warm winter nights to feed. They hunt along forest edges and over waterways.

### HOW TO SPOT

**Size:** Wingspan of 8 to 10 inches (20.3 to 25.4 cm); 0.14 to 0.3 ounces (4 to 8.5 g)

**North American Range:** Southeastern Canada, eastern United States, and eastern Mexico

**Habitat:** Forests

**Diet:** Caddisflies, moths, beetles, and other insects

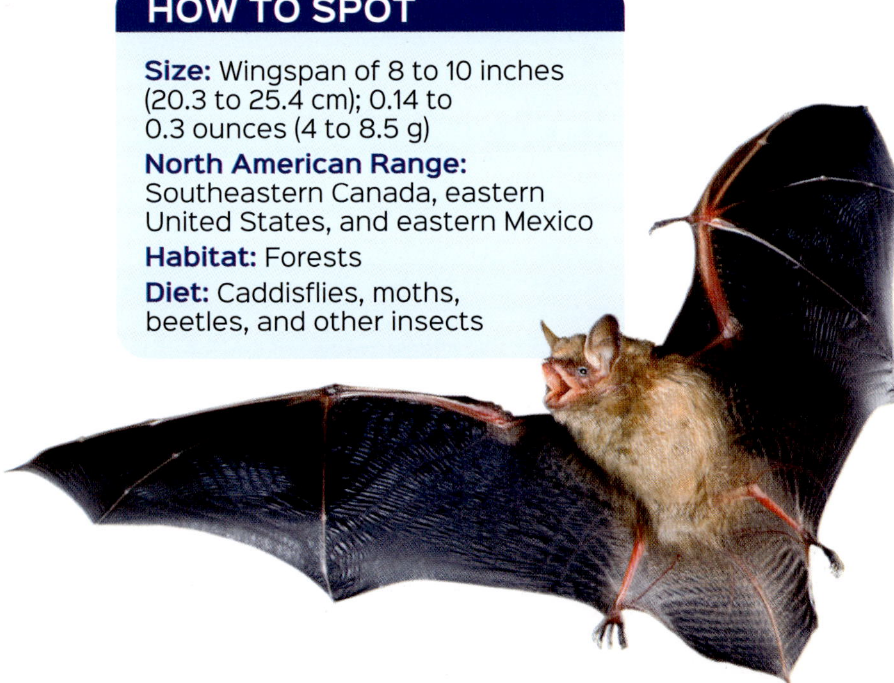

**FUN FACT**
The tricolored bat switches roosts often. But it also returns to the same sites year after year.

## RABIES

Rabies is a viral disease that damages the brain and spinal cord. In humans it causes seizures, hallucinations, and paralysis. The disease is often fatal once symptoms appear. Animal bites are the most common way to get rabies. Of rabies deaths in the United States, 70 percent are caused by bat bites. The virus from an infected animal enters a person's bloodstream. After coming in contact with a bat, it is important to seek medical treatment. Quick administration of a rabies vaccine is nearly 100 percent effective in preventing the disease from developing.

# WESTERN RED BAT

## *(LASIURUS BLOSSEVILLII)*

The western red bat shares a similar rusty-red color with the eastern red bat. However, the western red bat lacks a two-colored coat. The western red bat is also slightly smaller than the eastern red bat. The western red bat has short, rounded ears and a furred tail. These two species only overlap in western Texas.

## HOW TO SPOT

**Size:** Wingspan of 11 to 13 inches (27.9 to 33 cm); 0.3 to 0.5 ounces (8.5 to 14.2 g)

**North American Range:** Southwestern United States, Mexico, and Central America

**Habitat:** Forest edges

**Diet:** Insects

Western red bats hunt and migrate in groups that are usually separated by sex. Male and female western red bats have different summer ranges and migrate at different times. The western red bat mates in the fall, and fertilization is delayed until the spring. Females give birth to as many as five pups when food sources are plentiful. The western red bat chooses secluded roosts that offer protection against predators, including opossums and jays.

# WESTERN SMALL-FOOTED MYOTIS *(MYOTIS CILIOLABRUM)*

The western small-footed myotis has brown to pale yellow fur on its back. The fur on its belly is paler and can appear almost white in some populations. The bat has a black patch of fur across its eyes. It has dark ears and wings. This bat looks like the California myotis, but the western small-footed myotis has a larger skull.

## HOW TO SPOT

**Size:** Wingspan of 8.3 to 10 inches (21 to 25.4 cm); 0.2 to 0.3 ounces (5.7 to 8.5 g)

**North American Range:** South-central Canada to central United States

**Habitat:** Rocky areas near water

**Diet:** Moths, flies, beetles, and other small flying insects

The western small-footed myotis is an insectivore. In regions where both the western and California small-footed myotis occur, the western small-footed myotis tends to primarily eat beetles. This is an abundant food source because the California species mainly eats moths. The bat often roosts alone in rock crevices, caves, mines, and dead pine trees.

Maternity colonies are small, usually including between two and six individuals. Some females remain solitary even when nursing. They give birth to one pup a year. Pups are weaned after about five weeks.

# YUMA MYOTIS *(MYOTIS YUMANENSIS)*

The Yuma myotis is a small bat with light brown to dark brown fur that is paler on its belly. Its ears are short, glossy, and darkly colored. The bat's wings are also dark. It has a wide wingspan, which allows it to fly quickly around trees.

**FUN FACT**

In domed mines, the area of the roost may be 31 degrees Fahrenheit (17°C) warmer than the rest of the cavern from the body heat created by a colony of Yuma myotises.

## HOW TO SPOT

**Size:** Wingspan of 9.4 inches (23.9 cm); 0.2 to 0.3 ounces (5.7 to 8.5 g)

**North American Range:** Southwestern Canada, western United States, and western Mexico

**Habitat:** Near water in forests, grasslands, and deserts

**Diet:** Moths, mosquitoes, midges, and other insects

Yuma myotises often roost in buildings and under bridges in colonies that may include as many as 10,000 bats. These bats also roost in caves and abandoned mines. They leave their roost a couple of hours after sunset to forage for insects.

Yuma myotises mate before hibernation. Females give birth to one pup per year. The large size of maternity colonies helps keep pups warm. The Yuma myotis is one of the many bat species affected by white nose syndrome.

# GLOSSARY

**colony**
A group of animals of a particular species that hibernate or migrate together.

**coniferous**
A type of evergreen tree with needle-shaped leaves that produces seed cones.

**deciduous**
A type of tree that loses its leaves seasonally.

**forage**
To search for food.

**gestation period**
The typical length of a pregnancy, from conception until birth.

**insectivore**
An animal that eats insects.

**maternity colony**
A group of females of a particular species that roost together before and after giving birth.

**membrane**
A thin, flexible layer of skin or other tissue.

**monogamous**
Having one sexual partner.

**muzzle**
The protruding part of the face that typically includes the mouth and nose.

**pitch**
The highness or lowness of a sound.

**regurgitate**
To bring already-swallowed food back into the mouth.

**roost**
The place where bats shelter when resting.

**secrete**
To form and give off.

**semiarid**
Having only light rainfall.

**tragus**
The flap of skin in front of the ear.

**vertebrate**
A creature with a backbone.

**wean**
To begin to rely on food sources other than the mother's milk.

# TO LEARN MORE

## FURTHER READINGS

Drimmer, Stephanie Warren. *Ultimate Mammalpedia*. National Geographic Kids, 2023.

Mooney, Carla. *Mammals*. Abdo, 2026.

Riera, Lucas. *Nocturnal: Animals After Dark*. Gestalten, 2023.

## ONLINE RESOURCES

To learn more about North American bats, please visit **abdobooklinks.com** or scan this QR code. These links are routinely monitored and updated to provide the most current information available.

# PHOTO CREDITS

Cover Photos: Danita Delimont/Shutterstock Images, front (top left, upper middle, bottom right); Nilupa Dilshan/Shutterstock Images, front (top right); Shutterstock Images, front (upper left flying, middle right); McDonald Wildlife Photography Inc./Corbis/Getty Images, front (upper middle little); Beth Ruggiero-York/Shutterstock Images, front (upper middle wings up); Hal Brindley/Shutterstock Images, front (upper right front view); Martin Janca/Shutterstock Images, front (middle left); Rudmer Zwerver/Shutterstock Images, front (middle); Dennis W. Donohue/Shutterstock Images, front (bottom left); Hal Beral/Corbis/Getty Images, front (bottom middle); Natalia Kuzmina/Shutterstock Images, back (hanging); James Hager/robertharding/Getty Images, back (flying)
Interior Photos: John Abbott/NaturePL/Science Source, 1 (top left), 52 (top); MerlinTuttle.org/Science Source, 1 (top right), 1 (middle right), 3 (top left), 3 (top right), 3 (bottom), 4 (left), 4 (middle), 4 (right), 5 (top middle), 5 (bottom middle), 5 (bottom right), 6–7, 8 (left), 9, 10–11, 12, 12–13, 14, 17 (right), 19, 21, 22, 27, 29, 30, 33 (top), 34 (bottom), 37, 39, 40, 44, 50, 53, 54 (top), 56, 58, 59, 60–61, 61, 62, 64 (top), 66–67, 70, 71, 75, 77 (bottom), 78, 79, 80, 81, 84, 86, 88 (top), 90, 93, 94, 96–97, 98, 100, 102, 103, 106, 106–107, 112 (left), 112 (right), 112 (middle bottom); Danita Delimont/Shutterstock Images, 1 (middle left), 4–5, 32–33, 74–75, 82–83; NPS, 25 (top), 64 (bottom), 74, 104; Hal Brindley/Shutterstock Images, 3 (middle), 5 (bottom left), 31 (top); Anthony Mercieca/Science Source, 1 (bottom), 5 (top left), 48–49, 104–105; Gilbert S. Grant/Science Source, 5 (top right), 25 (bottom); Hila Taylor/iNaturalist, 6, 66; Shutterstock Images, 8 (right), 15 (bottom right), 26, 28 (bottom), 35, 36, 43, 49, 50–51, 57 (bottom), 77 (top), 96 (bottom), 99 (bottom); USFWS, 10; Paul Cryan/USGS, 11;

Leonardo Mercon/Shutterstock Images, 15 (top); Rudmer Zwerver/Shutterstock Images, 15 (bottom left); Wikimedia Commons, 16; Dr. Morley Read/ Shutterstock Images, 17 (left); John David Chenger/NPS, 18; Tereso Hernández Morales/ iNaturalist, 20; Alessandher Piva/iNaturalist, 23; Kristen Lalumiere/NPS, 24–25; Luciano Massa/iNaturalist, 28 (top); iNaturalist, 31 (bottom), 34 (top); Daniel Pineda Vera/iNaturalist, 33 (bottom); Andrew M. Snyder/ Moment/Getty Images, 38; Dr. Morley Read/Science Source, 41; Isaac Brown/Shutterstock Images, 42 (bottom); Michael Durham/Minden Pictures, 42 (top); Ernie Valdez/USGS, 45; Jay Ondreicka/Shutterstock Images, 46, 47 (bottom), 89; Dennis W. Donohue/ Shutterstock Images, 47 (top); Lauren Angel/BLM, 48; Erin Lynch/NPS, 52 (bottom); Red Line Editorial, 54 (bottom); Bacilio Ponce/Shutterstock Images, 55; Al Hicks/NYDEC/ USFWS, 57 (top); Emily Marie Wilson/Shutterstock Images, 60; Michael Durham/Nature Picture Library/Alamy, 62–63, 76–77; Eric Isselee/Shutterstock Images, 63; Ann Froschauer/USFWS, 65; Daniel Istvanko/Shutterstock Images, 68, 69 (top); Andrew King/USFWS, 69 (bottom); ER Degginger/Science Source, 72; Liz Weber/Shutterstock Images, 73; Max Faulkner/Fort Worth Star-Telegram/Tribune News Service/Getty Images, 82; Amanda Guercio/Shutterstock Images, 83; USDA, 85 (top); Gary Peeples/USFWS, 85 (bottom); Porter Libby/USDA, 87; Tony Tilford/Shutterstock Images, 88 (bottom); Pete Pattavina/ USGS, 91 (top); Larisa Bishop-Boros/KDFWR/USFWS, 91 (bottom); Juan Cruzado Cortés/ iNaturalist, 92; Phyllis Peterson/ Shutterstock Images, 95 (top); James Hager/robertharding/ Alamy, 95 (bottom); BLM, 97; Jeff Hajenga/USFWS, 99 (top); iStockphoto, 101; Daniel Neal/ Wikimedia Commons, 107

**ABDOBOOKS.COM**
Published by Abdo Reference, a division of ABDO, PO Box 398166, Minneapolis, Minnesota 55439. 

Printed in China.
102025
012026

Editor: Kari Cornell
Series Designer: Colleen McLaren
Production Designer: Tara Raymo

**LIBRARY OF CONGRESS CONTROL NUMBER: 2025939290**
**PUBLISHER'S CATALOGING-IN-PUBLICATION DATA**
Names: Lim, Angela, author.
Title: Bats / by Angela Lim
Description: Minneapolis, Minnesota: Abdo Reference, 2026 | Series: North American field guides | Includes online resources.
Identifiers: ISBN 9781098298944 (lib. bdg.) | ISBN 9798384932741 (ebook)
Subjects: LCSH: Bats--Juvenile literature. | Nocturnal animals--Juvenile literature. | Bats--Behavior--Juvenile literature. | Zoology--Juvenile literature. | Encyclopedias--Juvenile literature.
Classification: DDC 599.4--dc23